# CONTENTS

Some words are shown in bold, **like this**. You can find out what they mean by looking in the glossary.

# COULD I SIT ON A CLOUD?

No—you would fall through it! Clouds might look **solid**, but they are actually made of tiny **droplets** of water. These droplets are so light that they float in the air. Sometimes the droplets join together to make bigger drops. When these drops become too heavy to float, they fall as rain, sleet, or snow.

If clouds were solid, mountains could not poke through them!

# COULD ANYONE LIVE ON THE MOON?

In the 1960s and 1970s, astronauts traveled to the Moon. They stayed for about a day, but it would be tricky to live there for a long time. There is no air to breathe, no food to eat, and nowhere to live. But, if people could take enough of these things to the Moon with them, it might happen one day...

# IS IT THE SAME TIME ALL OVER THE WORLD?

No. When the Sun is highest in the sky, it is about midday. But because Earth is always spinning, midday happens at different times in different places. When it is breakfast time in the United States, it is lunchtime in Europe.

If we didn't have different **time zones**, some people might have to eat their lunch in the middle of the night!

# WHY DON'T I FALL OUT OF A ROLLER COASTER WHEN IT GOES UPSIDE DOWN?

When you are moving, your body wants to keep traveling in a straight line. But as a roller coaster enters a loop-the-loop, the track goes upward. Since your body cannot go forward anymore, you get pushed into your seat instead. As long as the force pushing you into your seat is greater than the force of **gravity**, you will not fall out!

# Did you know?

Roller coasters speed up as they plunge down huge slopes. This extra speed keeps the cars going all the way around loops like this one.

# WILL I EVER MEET AN ALIEN?

The truth is that no one knows. We might be alone in the universe. We might not. But there are many other stars that can support life, like the Sun supports life on Earth. There might be other planets like Earth going around these stars. So, it is possible there could be aliens living on some of them...

## Did you know?

There are hundreds of billions of stars in our **galaxy** and millions more galaxies beyond. So there are a LOT of stars out there!

# CAN I MAKE MY OWN CLOUDS?

Sort of! Your breath contains **water vapor**, but you do not usually see it. However, when you breathe out on a cold day, the water vapor meets cold air, cools, and turns into water **droplets**. A single water droplet is too small to see, but when there are lots of them together, they look like clouds.

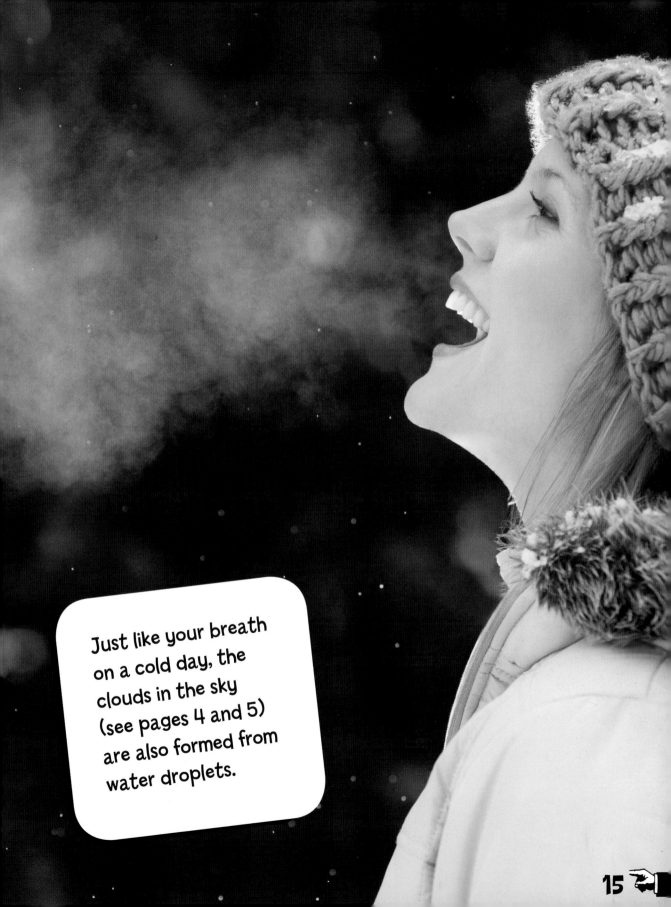

Just like your breath on a cold day, the clouds in the sky (see pages 4 and 5) are also formed from water droplets.

# WHY DOES MY ICE CREAM DRIP DOWN MY ARM?

It is because of **temperature**. When water freezes, it becomes ice, which is **solid**. When it warms, it becomes **liquid**. Ice cream contains water, so it stays solid in the freezer. But when you lick it on a sunny day, ice cream melts to become liquid.

## Did you know?

You can make your own ice cream by mixing cream, sugar, and egg together and then freezing it. Create your own flavors by adding mashed-up fruit.

# HOW DOES THE FIZZ GET INTO SODA?

Soda has a **gas** called carbon dioxide forced into it. Then, the soda is put into cans or bottles, and the gas is trapped inside. When the drink is opened, bubbles of carbon dioxide escape from the **liquid**. This gives the drink its fizz!

WARNING: Do not shake cans or bottles of soda. Carbon dioxide above the liquid will be **reabsorbed** into the drink, making it so fizzy that it explodes!

# WHY AREN'T BIRDS ELECTROCUTED WHEN THEY SIT ON WIRES?

Electricity always travels down to the ground if it can. Birds stay safe because their legs only touch the power line. If birds had legs so long that one foot touched the ground as well, then electricity would be able to travel along their leg and down to the ground—and the bird would get zapped!

BZZZT!

BZZZT!

21

# CAN I MAKE MY OWN RAINBOW?

Sort of! Light is made up of all the colors we see in a rainbow. When sunlight shines through raindrops, the different colors form a rainbow in the sky. You can create a similar effect by shining a light through a **prism**. This lets you see the rainbow colors in light.

A prism is a specially shaped piece of glass or clear plastic.

# DOES THUNDER EVER HAPPEN BEFORE LIGHTNING?

No, thunder always comes after lightning. Lightning happens when electricity jumps from cloud to cloud, or from a cloud down to the ground. Thunder is the sound that lightning makes. But because the speed of light is much faster than the speed of sound, we always see lightning before we hear it.

**Did you know?**
Light travels at 982 million feet per second. But sound only travels through air at 1,130 feet per second.

# IF EARTH IS SPINNING, WHY DON'T I FLY OFF INTO SPACE?

It is a force called **gravity** that stops you from taking off! Everything in the universe has gravity, but the bigger the object, the more gravity it has. Earth is very big, so it has a lot of gravity and pulls you toward it.

No matter how high we jump into the air, gravity always pulls us back down again with a bump!

# WHY CAN I SEE THE MOON IN THE DAYTIME?

The Moon **orbits** Earth all the time, not just at night. So, when the Moon is on our side of Earth in the daytime, we can sometimes see it. Stars shine during the day, too, but their light is much dimmer than sunlight, so we do not see them.

**Did you know?**
The Moon does not shine. Moonlight is actually light **reflected** from the Sun.

# GLOSSARY

**atmosphere** layer of gases around a planet

**droplet** very small amount of liquid

**galaxy** collection of stars and other matter held together by gravity

**gas** substance, such as air, that can move around freely

**gravity** force that pulls everything toward Earth

**liquid** runny substance, such as water

**orbit** go around and around something

**prism** solid shape with no curves, often with triangular ends

**reabsorb** take in or soak up something again

**reflect** bounce something back, usually light

**solid** hard or firm

**temperature** how hot or cold something is

**time zone** area on our planet where all the clocks are set to the same time

**water vapor** very tiny droplets of water

# FIND OUT MORE

## Books

Bell-Rehwoldt, Sheri. *Science Experiments That Surprise and Delight: Fun Projects for Curious Kids.* Mankato, Minn.: Capstone, 2011.

Brent Sandvold, Lynette. *Time for Kids Super Science Book.* New York: Time for Kids, 2009.

Harrison, Paul. *Space (Up Close).* New York: Rosen, 2008.

## Web sites

Facthound offers a safe, fun way to find Internet sites related to this book. All of the sites on Facthound have been researched by our staff.

Here's all you do:
Visit www.facthound.com
Type in this code: 9781410951991

# INDEX